When Famous People Come to Town

Essay Series

Also by Damien Wilkins

THE VETERAN PERILS *(stories, 1990)*

THE MISERABLES *(1993)*

THE IDLES *(poems, 1993)*

LITTLE MASTERS *(1996)*

NINETEEN WIDOWS UNDER ASH *(2000)*

CHEMISTRY *(2001)*

When Famous People Come to Town

Damien Wilkins

Series editor: Lloyd Jones

Four Winds Press
Wellington

© Damien Wilkins 2002

ISBN 0-9582375-3-0

First published September 2002

This book is copyright. Apart from
any fair dealing for the purpose
of private study, reasearch, criticism
or review, as permitted under the
Copyright Act, no part may be
reproduced by any process without
the permission of the publisher.

Design and typography by Catherine Griffiths
Typeset in Perpetua and Clarendon

Printed by Printlink

When Rudyard Kipling came in 1891 we almost missed him. The Wellington shipping reporter who posed his regular question, "Anybody worthwhile on board?", had never heard of the writer and decided to follow him up only when he came across another visitor to the ship – a local bookseller – seeking this Kipling out. There was a stroll along Lambton Quay and then a visit to the National Museum, where Kipling is supposed to have said, "Ah, here I am at home again amongst the dead bones and the ancient stones!"

We might pause here briefly to reflect on some shift; namely that the comic set-piece of encounters with foreigners, "What do you think of New Zealand?", is in danger of being replaced by another question, "What do you think of Te Papa?": a re-routing of some deftness since it suggests we have actually founded a national institution to house our anxieties – and one which opens on Sundays.

The visits of the famous are always connected with our anxieties.

The Wellington reporter was a horse-racing man and this was pre-*Jungle Book*, so he can't be blamed too much. Nevertheless Kipling's short stories – endorsed by Henry James – were known, and on his journey most of the major ports recognised Kipling's celebrity. He ate kiwi ("skin like pork crackling"), found Wellington full of "extraordinarily good-looking people with long eyelashes", and went out on a still harbour in a canoe rowed by "no less than ten beautiful maidens". It's difficult to know what to do with this traveller's bounty; there's so much to disbelieve, starting perhaps with the detail of the still harbour. For the theorist of fame, however, this two-page reminisce has another cargo – New Zealand brings the traveller close to a different kind of attraction:

I had some notion of sailing from Auckland to visit Robert Louis Stevenson at Samoa, for he had done me the honour to write me about some of my tales; and moreover I was Eminent Past Master R.L.S.

Fame famously attracts fame; it forms a club. Kipling had also called on Mark Twain in America the year before, leaving his card and his conversation – "talk," in Twain's words, "which might be likened to footprints, so strong and definite was the impression left behind". The great American wrote of the meeting: "Between us, we cover all knowledge; he knows all that can be known, and I know the rest." To complete this little circuit we should also note that Twain himself came to New Zealand four years after Kipling for a series of readings and lectures. He wrote on whatever took his fancy: moa bones, women's suffrage, dentures ("bad teeth in the colonies"), a lignified caterpillar with a plant growing out its back shown to him by Dr Hockin (sic) in Dunedin, which becomes a gleeful lesson in the cruelty of Nature, and, perhaps best of all, Twain reproduces a lengthy extract from the confession of one of the convicted killers involved in Nelson's "Maungatapu Murders".

Twain finds the document remarkable: "For brevity, succinctness, and concentration, it is perhaps without its peer in the literature of murder." (Here we are put in mind of Australian novelist Patrick White's interest in "a good New Zealandy murder".) The rate might be unremarkable but the style in which we kill each other seems to offer the outsider a contemplative satisfaction.

In any survey of writing by the famous about New Zealand, Twain's improper enthusiasms are a standout. The country's enthusiasm for him is expressed by a *New Zealand Mail* reporter as a kind of devotional hunger: "I don't care whether Mark be a good lecturer or not. It is the man I want to see and hear." Uncritical need sponsored by remoteness – we could easily replace Mark with Alfred or Edward or Elizabeth.

But we left Kipling in Auckland. Unfortunately, the

state of the fruit-boat captain ("devotedly drunk") persuades him to give up hope of seeing Robert Louis Stevenson and to return to India. Before that, however, Kipling finds in Invercargill ("the Last Lamppost in the World"), if not a replacement for R.L.S, then surely a beautifully rendered image of eminence as General Booth, founder of the Salvation Army, comes on board:

> I saw him walking backward in the dusk over the uneven wharf, his cloak blown upwards, tulip-fashion, over his grey beard, while he beat a tambourine in the face of the singing, weeping, praying crowd who had come to see him off.

Earlier in the piece, Kipling has expressed a sort of helplessness in the face of the favours his travelling life grants him: "One cannot repay the unrepayable by grins and handshakes." General Booth, walking backward with his tambourine, shows another way – the tactic repels Kipling (he remonstrates with the General later on their voyage); still the fiction writer grabs it. In Kipling's description, the scene is parodic, comic, absurd but also lovely, enlivened as it is not so much by the singing, weeping and praying crowd but by that detail of the uneven wharf.

*

Repaying the unrepayable is not a bad description of that means of coming to town favoured by royals – the tour.

Our first royal missed his connection. He was delayed in Australia – someone had tried to kill him there at a charity picnic – but when Alfred, Queen Victoria's second son, finally made it to New Zealand in 1869, his gunshot wounds all healed (ministered by two of Florence Nightingale's nurses: fame attracts itself), we showed him we could do leafy decorated arches as well as anyone. (Nine years earlier Montreal had set the standard with a fancy sort of hedge for his older brother Edward.) Alfred rode through our arches at Lyttelton and at Queen's Wharf, Wellington. In the photos it all looks terribly makeshift and dreary, a bit pantomime. Dirt roads, horse and carriages, men in hats, a sign saying Peace and Plenty – the perfect setting for a botched assassination.

Back in Sydney, James O'Farrell, the failed assassin with alleged Fenian connections, had been hanged six weeks after the attempt on the Prince's life. One day after the shooting, 20,000 Sydney-siders attended a public "indignation meeting". The whole colony, it was said, had been wounded in the person of its royal guest. We have never had to feel such a wound. What's on our conscience? A few eggs maybe, some vegetables, a pair of buttocks, otherwise our guests have gone unmolested. We need to turn to fiction to find anything different.

In Bill Manhire's story "Days of Sail", the Queen is visiting Dunedin in 1981. She looks out her window: "What a dump, she thinks. What a ghastly hole." As a kind of payback – not necessarily for regal contempt, since there are other less transparent reasons operating – an assassin prepares to spoil things. The narrator's parents have been killed in the Tangiwai Rail Disaster in 1953. They had been travelling to Auckland to see relatives: "They also hoped they might see the Queen there. They said they would tell her to look out for me when she got to Dunedin. They thought that was a great joke." In joining these two visits – the 1981 tour with the new Queen's first trip – the story seems to want to exact a kind of retribution. The earlier catastrophe will "make sense" once it is tied forever to that royal figure whose part in the rail disaster has been hitherto buried.

The gun does go off, but harmlessly – disaster averted with a New Zealandy flourish: a sheep butts the assassin just as she is taking aim. Perhaps even more distinctively *us* in its attitude towards royalty, however, is this family snapshot: "My aunt says that my mother said on the station platform that she needed a little fillip and my father said Elizabeth already had him."

*

It has always been the sickly triumph of the royal tour to provoke gratitude in the very people on whom it visits a costly humiliation. When Henry I travelled he required the host to supply wine for his horse's foot-bath. Every mile of road Elizabeth I went on had to be swept first. When George V went to Nepal in 1911, they put on 39 tigers for him to shoot, of which the royal bag was 24. Of course it's not all one-way traffic. King James I couldn't stop handing out knighthoods, creating so many in such a short space of time that he is said to have once conferred the title with the words, "Arise Sir What-You-Will". The current Duke of Edinburgh supplies the appropriately banal contemporary parallel of such forgetful and meaningless largesse. Opening a new annex to Vancouver City Hall in 1969, he says: "I declare this thing open – whatever it is."

Hence the truth of the royal tourist – they didn't know where they were, unless they were handed a gun. If it's a kangaroo in the sights, then this must be . . . a grizzly bear means the other place . . . the Uganda kob means . . . When the Queen Mother came in 1958 we gave her a fishing rod, a pair of waders and all of Lake Wanaka. There probably wasn't much slaughter that day and not much since. A trawl through the photographic archive uncovers the diminishment. The trade and industry component of such visits has imposed itself on the itinerary so that now royal blood-lust gets sensitively channelled into . . . the farm visit.

In a memorably boring series of photos recording Philip's visit to a Canterbury dairy farm in 1956, we slowly grasp the bovine intelligence behind the initiative. The Duke stands in a milking shed, hands behind his back, head slightly inclined towards the farmer who is speaking, presumably, about milking cows. There is not a single molecule – animal or mineral, commoner or other – which does not cry out from this tableau: "Let me be!" The farmer trapped in his suit and the Duke trapped in his pose of fascination are as securely tied to machinery of the visit as the cows to the milk pumps – everyone is grabbed by the teats.

The priceless image, however, is an "off-duty" shot of Philip and a cow standing with their rears facing the camera. It's hard to say why this picture is so appealing and so essential to our study of fame. Man and beast, one thinks — their job done but their labours stretching on.

The inspection of animal flesh seems an inescapable royal duty. (Philip also went to the Gear Meatworks in Petone for a chin-wag with some splattered subjects — a bit more manly than milking.) It should be no surprise that horses are high on the list of watched animals. The notion of the thoroughbred — inheritance through breeding — must always be joined to the tour. This accounts for the odd preference our visitors have shown over the years for Trentham Racetrack, a place one might feel affection for in a proportion directly inverse to any "fineness". Trentham is not pretty. It is not regal. It isn't actually very nice. But it is a racetrack and there are horses and so they've come: in 1934 (Duke of Gloucester), in 1954 (Queen and Duke), in 1958 (Queen Mother), and so on. And when they're there we get them to hand out things to winners ("Arise Sir What-You-Will").

Now a racetrack, in its divisions – members from others, winner's circle from track, large-bet window from regular, women in hats from women holding babies – lends itself rather easily to a bit of class analysis. (What such analysis might yield is less clear; a doctor or lawyer might easily be found in the "public" area and a plumber in the members'.) Nevertheless, every punter is sharply aware that this is a demarcated space he moves through, and that there are privileges on offer for a price – a royal locus then, despite any shabbiness.

Nor is it only "real" royalty that makes use of such a venue. In the early '90s the racetrack hosted the Prime Minister and his wife and Rod Stewart and his. They sat together in the members' stand. Father of nine, conservative Catholic Jim Bolger, sat beside Randy Rod, father of the paternity suit. And Joan next to Rachel. (The struggle to bring that afternoon's conversations into focus must finally be a doomed one, though many present were surely working at it.) There was a lot of looking from the races up into the stand, from the horses up at the flesh. When Rachel Hunter walked among us, drawing our eye from the birdcage, we understood the lesson. She had, it seemed, an equine power. She was a thoroughbred and a winner: royalty.

In *Henry V*, the English King despatches his ambassador to the French palace with a document proving Henry's line of descent back to the feared Edward:

He sends you this most memorable line,
In every branch truly demonstrative;
Willing you overlook this pedigree:
And when you find him evenly derived
From his most famed of famous ancestors,
Edward the Third, he bids you then resign
Your crown and kingdom, indirectly held
From him the native and true challenger.

Henry V out of My Kingdom by way of Gizza Crown.

A newspaper report on the southern leg of the Duke of York's 1927 New Zealand visit supplies further evidence of the cross-over between royalty and horses. The *Press* offers a commentary on the party's progress through Dunedin streets – a route "thickly lined with people" – as it nears the finish line:

> They certainly took a keen interest in what was passing, and at times raised cheers, but it was not until the procession was nearing the Club that anything in the nature of hearty cheering was heard, and then such cheering came from a

> party of High School girls. There was indeed throughout the southern tour a most marked restraint in the matter of vocal salutation . . .

It is noted that the royal guest is "bearing up wonderfully": "many people were surprised to notice how fresh and alert he was to-day after his big day in Christchurch on Tuesday". A stayer then. But such a race schedule exacts its price: "Regret was everywhere expressed that the health of the Duchess had broken down under the strain of the tour."

In Ashburton, the Duke had been greeted by an arch with an innovation: two carcasses of Canterbury lamb were suspended from its pillars, and cheese and butter were also "prominent in the scheme". There is no record of other towns emulating the edible arch. The Duke has located his audience's weak spot: "I congratulate you," he announces in the letter he leaves the town (oddly, it is read aloud by the mayor as the train pulls out), "on the fertility of your soil."

In following our minor theme of fame's solicitous nature, we should also acknowledge the story of Zane Grey, who at the time of the Duke's visit was a sort of one-man tourism department for the Far North. Grey offered the Duke the use of his fishing launches while in Russell. Internal Affairs botched the offer or at least failed to tell the famous writer of Westerns that his boats would not be required. Grey stewed in Russell for a few hours. No one from the Duke's ship, the *Renown*, made any overtures. Grey felt the snub, which was in turn felt by the local MP who was taking it up with the government so that "satisfactory explanation" could be made: "Personally he regretted that any annoyance had been caused a distinguished American citizen like Mr Grey, who by his writing had done much and was doing much to advertise New Zealand."

There is something yet to be picked off the bones of that newspaper report from Dunedin — and it's something similar to the taste of that Manhire assassination attempt story: "a most marked restraint in the matter of vocal salutation". We'll gather in thick crowds but we won't be going crazy. (That'll only be those silly schoolgirls.) We shall attend at the appointed time of the drive-by or the walkabout and agree whenever prompted that he is a jolly good fellow, but it will be curiosity – the kind of stupefied sense of expectation that shuttles the emotions of a crowd between tension and boredom, hope and anxiety, longing and disappointment – holding us in our lines.

Now might be the time to think a little about what it is that is exported in the shape of a royal visit. What are we getting exactly?

Whenever some royal event happens in Britain, we can prepare ourselves for the journalist's stand-by that "pageantry is what the British do best". Like the bloom on all compliments, it carries the dew of insult. Once there was an Empire and now there's a few fancy carriages left. What is celebrated on the Mall these days – and this accounts for its occasional poignancy – is vestige.

When the Londoner, recently interviewed for radio, says that he's come for the Golden Jubilee because he first saw the royal carriage in 1947 and he thought he'd like another look at it, he articulates that need we have to see our lives expressed in physical shapes along a timeline: schools, houses, children, cars, whatever. (This is something of what people mean when they make that strange claim that they are attending a public event because they want to be "part of history" – the event makes visible what is usually unseen; not the one-off of the event so much as the perpetual, indiscernible motion of their lives.) The Londoner is watching his old Queen and he is watching her younger self too, just as standing in 2002 he has a sudden view of himself as the young man who stood on the Mall just after the war. It isn't easy to throw off the suggestive power of such moments. How else to account for the way otherwise intelligent people grant the Queen the revered "common touch" simply on account of her ability to shake a few hands and pause for a moment for pleasantries?

Witness the British woman whom the TV cameras found after one recent walkabout. The Queen had actually talked to her. And how did the conversation go? "I said I saw you in 1953 and she said, Oh did you." Thus the rumour of her touch does grow.

Here is the helpless record of another meeting:

> Much of our conversation was about her son, Prince Charles, who had had his tonsils out only that morning. As soon as he recovered from anaesthetic, she said, he asked for ice cream as a reward and since then he had twice again wanted ice cream.

The memoirist is another famous visitor to New Zealand – Eleanor Roosevelt, writing in her autobiography. Eleanor made a war-time visit here, a morale-booster for US troops in the Pacific and a pacifying gesture to those hosting them. Interestingly, she had two goes at the New Zealand part of her reminiscences. In the later *On My Own* she cuts a passage that appears in *This I Remember* detailing a conversation she had about Maori children stealing food. She is rebuked by Rangi, her

Maori host: "which I deserved and I wished fervently I could be certain that the teaching of our children was always so successful, success evidently being a foregone conclusion so far as the Maoris were concerned." This passage, which she chooses no longer to remember, is difficult to decode. It may have been the reek of piety that caught her second time around. The other reading would position the offending note as sarcasm. Certainly she isn't afraid of displaying exasperation with her hosts, who are always claiming that any fish or game imported from the United States grows bigger here than there – a note of boastfulness worth returning to later. (For now we note that Anthony Trollope was saying the same sort of thing in 1875, though then it was Englishness which was improved on in the local setting: "He [the New Zealander] tells you that he has the same climate – only somewhat improved; that he grows the same produce – only with somewhat heavier crops; that he has the same beautiful scenery at his doors – only somewhat grander in its nature . . .")

Whatever the case, Eleanor Roosevelt is better at Rangi and at the voices of the Marines she meets than she is at finding what is memorable in her later conference with Elizabeth II. Between these two "historical" figures, the tonsil talk is almost a parody of emptiness. Now the Queen can hardly be blamed for the appearance of her bland chat in a book, and if she goes out of her way not to say interesting things to strangers, we can only remark that it seems to have worked for her.

What is memorable about people's encounters with the Queen is the anomalous position in which their reports place them. They are instantly in the grip of that dreadful thing, full recall. They do not edit the Queen, as we edit everyone. They let her speak: it is a fearful enchantment. And they themselves — except for their testifying voices — disappear.

*

We've finally come across the word which haunts all discussion of the royals so we'd better use it defini-

tively: a royal event in New Zealand is really an exercise in anomaly. Everyone knows this. Not because of republican fervour but because of circumstance and resources and temperament and geography and architecture and custom. We attempt pomp at our peril. This is not to say we are more "real" than the British, or that we are less deluded than they are because we don't have a palace, but perhaps we can say that our fantasies – for the visits of famous people also seem connected with those – have been shaped by our different histories.

In Bill Manhire's story we are asked to imagine the Queen taking snapshots of local highlights: "a haka party goes by on the deck of a lorry. *Snap*." She is also being briefed on our achievements by "some man" who tells her that she is visiting a city of firsts. The first woollen mills, 1874. The first daily newspaper, 1861. This nifty reversal – the forcing of our noteworthiness on her – might seem to offer a corrective to the ghastly imbalance of present relations, administering a blow to royal pre-eminence. But the story works somewhat differently from this. To make sense of the tone of the writing, it is necessary to understand that a fact such as "the first secondary school for girls" is a joke. To formulate the lesson in a way the fiction never does, the Queen is bad for us not because she makes us dismally submissive but because she makes us dismally *active*. She makes us the victim of our own boosterism, and draws from our feelings of inferiority the spectre of our vanity and pride. In such a mood we are likely to do anything – sling a couple of lamb carcasses up at Ashburton Railway Station; claim we have bigger fish than you, better scenery.

The photographic archive of royal visits to New Zealand is finally a collection of certain national awkwardnesses. Some of these are straightforwardly related to physical place – the crowds in 1954 look wrong because they are at Pukekura Park and they are watching the Queen and the Duke travel in a jeep.

For the deeper strangeness we might turn to the most pathetic of the "tribute" photos: an image from the Queen Mother's 1958 visit. The place is Wakari Hospital, outside Dunedin. On an expanse of concrete in front of the modern hospital buildings a group of patients has been gathered. In fact a little ward has been simulated, though it is an impossible one, a fantastic offering – some of every kind of sickness. For here we are in the realm of the irrational. There is a baby in a cot, there are children in beds and adult patients in beds, and a couple in wheelchairs, all plonked down and told to wait. A few nurses are there, making sure of things. There is no shade; one imagines it is hot. The concrete beams. It is a truly desolate scene. The arrangement of "a memorable day" has seldom seemed merciless. The Queen Mother has not come yet. It is often said of photographs that they capture a moment; here the moment is stretched and stretched. You feel the patients might still be there waiting. And in the anonymous face of the hospital building, poking from a window, we can almost summon the sniper's rifle . . .

*

Hostility toward the famous — there should be a study of it which sorts through the different grades of resistance and aggression. When famous people come to town, we can make all sorts of crazy demands of them, and usually they accede. We can easily coax a foolish pose for the camera — that must be our hostility, surely?

There's a photo taken during Anna Pavlova's 1926 tour. She is boarding a train, or has just got off a train, and she is standing in front of a flock of sheep who have come to meet the prima ballerina, or to

see her off, or ask her whether she prefers *Une Soirée de Chopin* to *The Fairy Doll* — we don't know why they're there; they're sheep. Maybe they've just wandered by and stopped the train in its tracks.

Here is another scenario from the opportunist's file. Christchurch, 1951. Backstage. The world's most famous violinist draws breath after the intensities of the Brahms D minor sonata. He still has the Bartok and the Kreutzer to go. There is a knock. (Maybe not even a knock; maybe not even a door.) Anyway, someone is standing there with his notebook and pen. Could there just be, before you go back on, a couple of quick questions, maestro?

Now let the *Press* tell it, the writer of the piece casting himself in the third person:

> It was no trouble, said Mr Yehudi Menuhin, with a pleasant smile, when a reporter apologised for interrupting him during the interval of his concert last evening in the Theatre Royal. After an hour's playing the great violinist was courteous and unruffled. He sat down to rest for a few minutes and answered questions.

The "pleasant smile" is good – we want to paint in the gritted teeth. Yet perhaps it's only a marker of our cynical relationship with fame and the famous that we now read Menuhin's courtesy as forbearance. The great violinist is asked about his itinerary (Wellington, Dunedin, Auckland, Sydney, Philadelphia, New York, "and one in Hollywood on Thursday fortnight" – a list, we might say, which begins in geography and ends in fantasy). He is asked about "modern composers" (quite a lot of good music written by them, he says, which doesn't quite dispel the question's inference — namely, we'd prefer if you didn't play that awful Bartok).

Then a question about local fancies ("Yesterday morning Mr Menuhin had expressed a desire to eat some South Island oysters"). Here the pleasantness is finally under pressure: "Last evening he said he had not yet had them. 'They have been promised for the day after tomorrow. An expedition is going out to get them.'" History has not recorded the fate of this expedition, and Menuhin, in his autobiography written 25 years after the visit, is also silent on the oysters.

Finally the violinist signals that this surprise interval interview is over by picking up his Strad and playing what the reporter calls "a jaunty little passage".

This encounter tempts us in a certain direction. We might feel that Menuhin has been disarmed by the Kiwi pluck of the *Press* reporter. The dressing-room break-in seems to suggest something of our attitude towards the great — that they are just like you and me, always happy for a bit of a yarn. (Of course to attempt an interview with the 1951 All Blacks at half-time might have rearranged such a notion.)

The "serious" review of the concert, which appears across the page from the interview, would see itself as well above such democratising tactics, but in fact it offers the genteel version of the same idea. The music critic, having described the "tumultuous reception" given to Yehudi and Hephzibah Menuhin, writes that "Mr Menuhin has for many years been on those eminent heights of fame where his surname alone has been, throughout the world, a hallmark of exquisite playing." Further on, however, the reviewer complains that the recital programmes — there were two concerts — had not been made available, so it had been impossible to make an informed choice about which one to attend. This failure indicates the abiding philistinism of the promoters: "One feels sure that both these players would be the first to admit that the music is of the greater importance than the performers, and would not entirely appreciate an advertising system which invites the public to hear great artists rather than great music."

Though these words come from 1951, this is really the voice of the '40s, the voice of asperities and hardships and rationing; in short the voice of the war: stoic, dour, grudging, and – after the difficult Bartok has passed – willing to concede a communal, martial fever caused by Beethoven: ". . . and the whip of the wind in the exhilarating gallop of the last movement roused all present to add their acclaim to these artists who have been acclaimed by millions of hearers".

This is also a voice that must know the hope it utters is forlorn. The "advertising system" which promotes the performer over the performed has been flourishing for about two decades in a certain place in southern California. Look across the newspaper to the interview. Yehudi Menuhin has a gig there on Thursday fortnight.

Three years before, this same critic would have had the opportunity to be prescient all over again, with the visit to New Zealand of Heathcliff and Scarlett O'Hara, or Lord Admiral Nelson and Lady Hamilton, or whoever this "stellar couple" had just been in whatever movie was then playing. Just as Menuhin's celebrity was made decent by its cloak of Bach and Beethoven, so Laurence Olivier and Vivien Leigh appeared in the highly respectable garments of the Old Vic Theatre Company. It hardly dents that venerable institution – or Olivier's theatrical pedigree – to suggest the punters came first for the great and then for the great art.

A Neville Lodge cartoon from the time gives the game away. Two gents are entering the Stock Exchange (read: home of philistine businessmen). One is asking the other if he'd like to swap tickets. He's got test rugby seats and he wants to go to the Old Vic. Not very funny, but not bad as shorthand for a prevailing social mood. The Old Vic was a hot item and for all those affecting to be scandalised by the garish movie stuff, there was Sheridan's *The*

School for Scandal. For everyone else, there they were – him and her in the flesh.

But we hadn't finished with Yehudi. Picture that long flight heading towards the last gig, the last stop on the line, the final wave. Hello New Zealand! The famous are coming to town. One imagines them – though not Menuhin – dozing, a little drunk maybe, a bit zonked and shattered, a little assaulted in the way planes assault you, even forward of Economy.

We know that Yehudi Menuhin would always seek to profit by this downtime; he would "prepare" for countries en route. On his way to Tokyo in 1951 ("two days flying from San Francisco"), the violinist spent hours practising with chopsticks, "achieving a measure of competence and greatly amusing my Japanese hosts". It is not recorded if he amused his New Zealand hosts that same year with a little demonstration of something local – a haka? a spot of shearing? He'd wanted those oysters and they hadn't turned up. He did, however, have an experience here which "struck with the force of a revelation".

Waiting in an Auckland osteopath's rooms – the violinist was "another Western body knotted through and through" – Menuhin picks up a book on yoga. Immediately he feels he is holding "a key to unlock old enigmas", and he borrows the book for the duration of the tour: "All that week, when not travelling, rehearsing and performing, I shut myself up in various hotel rooms . . . finding much pleasure in exercises which demanded no strain but on the contrary inner quietness." (Inner quietness – how the phrase rebukes our friend the *Press* reporter.) Menuhin then prepared for India by practising yoga. By the time he got there he could stand on his head.

That seems the traveller's tale *par excellence*. The accidental find; the unguided memorable moment; the rule of all special journeys that only what is *not* on the itinerary will yield significance, everything else being tourism. It might also be the *famous* traveller's tale in miniature. Insulated from the actual, "shut up" in concert halls and hotel rooms, with occasional forays into the world to find medicinal and other remedies for such an afflicted life, the famous person's only inquiry is into their own dissatisfactions: the bad bed and the terrible food and The People One Meets.

When the famous report back on us, they strike certain themes; certain figures are always stepping forward. The bourgeois wife with a bruising sense of her own cultural credentials is stock. When Igor Stravinsky ("I.S.") visited in 1961, his assistant Robert Craft kept a diary:

> Reception by United States Ambassador Akers. Two hundred hands to shake – those of other ambassadors, the New Zealand Prime Minister, many members of pahlamint. Large N.Z. lady: "Well, frankly, Mr. Stravinsky, I like the Firebird best of all your works." I.S.: "And what a charming hat you have." . . . Wife of N.Z. dignitary: "Do you like architecture, Mr Stravinsky?" I.S.: "Let me think about it."

Noel Coward, recalling his visit to Wellington in 1940, finds a precedent for such aggression in the person of the Mayoress:

> She said to me in ringing tones that I was never to dare to sing "The Stately Homes of England" again as it was an insult

to the homeland and that neither she nor anybody else liked it. I replied coldly that for many years it had been one of my greatest successes, whereupon she announced triumphantly to everyone in earshot: "You see – he can't take criticism!" Irritated beyond endurance I replied that I was perfectly prepared to take intelligent criticism at any time, but I was not prepared to tolerate bad manners. With this I bowed austerely and left the party.

Both accounts are also battling the Antipodean Calvin. The mayoral reception for the famous English dramatist is preceded by a fight over whether his play can be broadcast in its entirety because of some risqué lyrics: "Because I detest aggressive puritanism, or any kind of puritanism, this flung me into a rage . . . the battle raged for several hours and I was ultimately victorious."
Stravinsky's entourage – a matter of a few years before the Beatles checked in to the same hotel – have no difficulty in identifying the source of this repressive shadow, though here it is not artistic freedom at stake but something more urgent:

> No danger of our stomachs being out to the test in the St. George Hotel. It maintains the poorest fare in the world

and the most puritanical code. Visitors may call only at prescribed hours, as at a reformatory, and by suffering the same suspicion. Wine, available in no city restaurants, can be obtained in the hotel, but only by registered guests who are willing to be regarded as depraved. And the day is as rule-ridden as a boarding school. Coffee is not served at night, but only tea, and the other way around at noon. And unless a special placard is attached to one's door, one is inundated at daybreak with a clattering service of compulsory tea.

When Australian rock group The Birthday Party came to Wellington in 1983, they were put in the dingy Cambridge Hotel – a fact that hardly registered. Nick Cave's only complaint was that they hadn't managed to find any drugs in the city. The band had just come from Berlin, so the loss was a keen one.

Craft, Coward and Cave are mining that tradition of traveller's tales which we might call Quaint Customs. The less interesting Balanced Report would include the fact that Stravinsky – at the time perhaps the most famous classical composer in the world – had invited himself, having heard about a quality national orchestra. He conducted a single performance of his work and then asked why more concerts hadn't been scheduled. His hosts reminded him that these had been his instructions. "But," said Stravinsky, "I didn't know that they are so good." He went back to the hotel where he failed to secure his dinner-time whisky. Naturally, Craft's diary would rather attempt its phonetic satire ("pahlamint") than be fair.

Similarly, our deficiency in narcotics that week day 20 years ago in Wellington masked another phenomenon — we were the only nation in the world to give punk group The Fall a number one hit with their raucous, stripped-down ode to impairment, "Totally Wired". Immediately everything else on the Top Ten seemed like so much "official" music. There may not have been drugs on every street corner but clearly there was a constituency, shading into the mainstream, prepared to tolerate alteration. It was a rogue result of course, and normal service was soon resumed; however, rogue results are something like a forté.

*

We are also rogue on the map. Being farthest out, we can take a Plutonian pride in our placement, and as the last stop on the line (Last Lamppost in the World) we attract the sort of interest that sends people to John O'Groats. For if the visits of famous people are our fantasies, we are also theirs. *The New Yorker* recently chose to explain New Zealand to its readers in these terms: "*The Lord of the Rings* was shot in New Zealand, a paradise still largely devoid of people."

Of course we are not quite the last stop. That privilege belongs to Antarctica, in whose narrative we take if not a leading role then a pivotal one – we are the hub in all South Polar itineraries . . . the portal to the ice. As such, we live in Captain Robert Falcon Scott's prose as paragon: "New Zealand welcomes us as its own, and showered on us a wealth of hospitality and kindness which assuredly we can never forget, however difficult we may have found it to express our thanks."

When Scott sets out from Lyttelton on the *Discovery*, there is more showering: "the afterpart of the deck was occupied by a terrified flock of forty-five sheep, a last and most welcome present from the farmers of New Zealand". The welcome present, however, threatens to interfere with the running of the ship: "Amidst this constantly stampeding body stood the helmsman at the wheel; further forward were sacks of food, and what space remained was occupied by our twenty-three dogs in a wild state of excitement." Scott shoulders the mayhem with typical poise, finally conceding that "As may be imagined, the ship was not in a condition in which one could look forward with pleasure to crossing the stormiest ocean in the world."

The crowds that came to see off Scott on both his expeditions were Empire crowds but they weren't dupes. Did they feel themselves to be, in some part, an extension of imperial power? Perhaps. They were also applauding and assisting in a project that involved enormous practical demands. (Scott takes some time to praise the various tradespeople who donated their services free of charge.) Indeed the obsessive calculating of supplies and provisions for the journey ahead – the intense domesticity of preparations – makes this "famous person event" singularly approachable.

At the wharf in 1901 and again in 1910, we are being asked to participate in an attempt at a feat of endurance and strength – that is, we are cheering *a thing we can see being done*: look, the ship is leaving, those are our sheep on board. Our witness is vivid and purposeful. Compare the wait to catch a glimpse of some royal's wave or some star's smile – there we receive, in the publicist's argot, an aura, a nothing. Nor are the 45 sheep on board the symbolic or silly sheep that were posed around Pavlova's knees, or the wasteful sheep hung from Lyttelton's arches to welcome Alfred: Scott's sheep are working sheep, team members – actually supper; in short, fuel.

It might be said that we've come in our crowds to be part of history – but to be in its engine room, please, rather than on its temporary viewing platform.

*

Famous writers, of course, tend to be aura-free, or at least they seldom inspire scenes of hysteria or gifts of livestock. When D.H. Lawrence berthed at Wellington in 1922, it is not known whether any horse-racing newspaperman posed the question, "Anyone worthwhile on board?" Lawrence used his day there to send his old friend and enemy, Katherine Mansfield, a one-word card: "Ricordi" (remembrances). He was in her home town. They'd fallen out badly and in his previous letter he had said, "You are a loathsome reptile – I hope you will die."

In Australia before that, Lawrence believed he now understood Mansfield and her sort. He didn't elucidate, though one passage in his letters sounds strikingly like Mansfield:

> The minute the night begins to go down, even the towns, even Sydney, which is huge, begins to feel unreal, as if it were only a daytime imagination, and in the night it did not exist. That is a queer sensation: as if the life here really had never entered in; as if it were just sprinkled over, and the land lay untouched.

Here is Mansfield's image from her story "The Woman at the Store", a kind of colonial murder ballad in which the social isolation of rural life breeds despair and violence:

> There is no twilight in our New Zealand days, but a curious half-hour when everything appears grotesque – it frightens – as though the savage spirit of the country walked abroad and sneered at what it saw.

Evening comes and everything changes, goes weird . . . you can't order whisky or coffee – that's the comic end of this same scale. At the poetic end, it's not hard to trace the influence of Mansfield's sneering half-hour on New Zealand painters, filmmakers and writers. The "savage spirit" is the default setting on any number of renditions of our landscape, both physical and mental, from Colin McCahon and Ngaio Marsh to James K. Baxter and Jane Campion. Lawrence's version of colonial unreality diverges from Mansfield's not in kind exactly but in terms of its potential usefulness. For the Englishman who hates England and travels the world perpetually frustrated in his search for somewhere to live ("I sort of wish I could go to the moon," he writes in 1929 from France), Australia – and by extension its neighbour – is a place where "human life seems to me very barren: one could never make a novel out of these people, they haven't got any insides to them, to write about." As if to prove himself right, he finished the first draft of *Kangaroo* while living there.

Mansfield did locate our "insides", yet she remains a matter of deep ambivalence to us.

She is a famous person who left town and never came back. Of course she got ill and died. Yet her absence can still figure as a rebuke. (By the time her father wrote his memoirs, he could boast that he'd been back and forth to England 24 times.) Irrationally, then, we feel abandoned, but also rather pleased her greatest works – "Prelude" and "At the Bay" – depend on the spurned place. Moreover, her value to us lies exactly in this strain. For the way Mansfield resists our claims of ownership, our instinct for pathetic gratitude, makes her an exemplary figure. We think twice before prostrating ourselves in front of this phantom.

Of course the invitation is there: KM, in a sense, *is* back in town, and there may be no better means of registering the strain and resistance she embodies than to visit her birthplace – the house in Thorndon, Wellington, which is kept as a museum.

It is hard to know at what point precisely on the tour the penny drops; perhaps it is on seeing the *Waverly* novels in the book cabinets or the fruit-cake on the dining table or the dolls in the children's bedroom upstairs. At some moment the house gives up its secret: this is all the stuff Mansfield ran screaming from. The fact that family love became her great subject should not soften our tread along the hallway of her first home, or prevent us from understanding that what is on display replicates all that was anathema to the writer.

"I just long for power over circumstances," the young Mansfield wrote in Wellington. It's a desire which has usually been read retrospectively, that is, as if the writer already spoke the words from behind a blood-spattered handkerchief – from within her tragic aura, as it were. It does us good to remember that around the time she made the pronouncement, the longing for power was expressed in such acts as wearing brown to match the colour of her beloved cello, and punching her best friend if that friend talked to another girl.

In her later recreation of a New Zealand childhood Mansfield trampled expertly on the Victorianisms of "model behaviour", and in the process did something of extraordinary and lasting influence for the culture: she linked youth not with promise but with its extinction. Childhood was torment and trauma but it was also as good as it was going to get. Adults were really just overgrown children. In fact, it is as if no one in Mansfield's fiction can grow up because there is nothing to grow up *into*. Now *that*, for better or worse, is a very New Zealandy theme.

*

This detour through Katherine Mansfield gives us purchase finally on those figures who swell every crowd when famous people come to town: the children. They come, of course, under duress mostly. A child's imaginative life usually demands something a bit more interesting than waiting around for an adult they don't know to show up. They come then, under Mansfield's matrix, not only to behave as little adults with their flags and their salutes – not only to *be* mimics – but also to *see* mimics: adults behaving like children.

Or if not that, which sounds too harsh after all, then we come as children and adults to feel for a moment caught up in a kind of half-willed disorientation, the crowd's collective dream of uplift, its trembling sense of occasion, its pride finally not in the person awaited but in itself – its size and its sound and the drama it generates by simply gathering on that day.

*

As children in 1971 we were taken to Trooping the

Colour. It was a hot June day. We stood for hours outside Buckingham Palace. What do I remember? The waiting, the crowds, the heat – nothing at all of the trooping. Nothing of the polished regiments and whatever else went past eventually. Horses, surely – though nothing of the pooping. Nothing of the famous person whose official birthday we were observing. But I remember this, we all do: a man fainting. He fell back into the crowd. Someone's fainted! Give him some room! Get back, get back! Someone's fainted!

To see someone faint is a special shock. Eerily, the person seems to have vanished, to have fallen back out of himself as it were. Soon the fainter will be identified as such (and not as the victim of something more sinister). He'll come round. Inhabit himself once more. Probably apologise for the fuss. You fainted, we'll explain. You just fainted. Have some water.

Someone is cradling his head, someone is holding his elbow. Someone is explaining what has happened to someone who didn't see. The site of the fainting is busy with employment and importance.

And the fainter – one more piece of thanks we owe him – will have made the day memorable, will have given it a distinct human weight: the weight of his body falling backwards but also the weight of our attendance on him, the details of our helping him and of his miraculous, ordinary recovery.

What happened in 1971 was this: slowly, the fainting man got to his feet and moved among us, shaking our hands, earnest and shaken and sheepish and happy. In years to come we'll again tell each other the story about the man who fainted in the crowd. That was the day the famous person came to town, remember.

*

Page 18: Crowd gathered in Wellington at the visit of the Duke and Duchess of Cornwall and York to New Zealand, 1901
George Moore Collection, Alexander Turnbull Library, National Library of New Zealand, Te Puna Matauranga o Aotearoa, G-65210-1/2

Page 28: A decorated arch to welcome Prince Alfred, Duke of Edinburgh, 1869 Auckland Public Library

Page 32: Anna Pavlova, 1926, during her visit to New Zealand
Alexander Turnbull Library, National Library of New Zealand, Te Puna Matauranga o Aotearoa, F-089575-1/2

Page 55: His Royal Highness Prince Edward, the Prince of Wales, tips his hat to the crowd in Wellington, 1920
K A Stewart Collection, Alexander Turnbull Library, National Library of New Zealand, Te Puna Matauranga o Aotearoa, F-57604-1/2